Greetings from Cincinnati

Mary L. Martin &
Dinah Roseberry

4—Fountain Square and Carew Tower at Night, Cincinnati, Ohio

Good Samaritan Hospital, Cincinnati, Ohio

VIEW OF CINCINNATI RIVER FRONT TAKEN FROM KENTUCKY SHORE.

UNION CENTRAL LIFE INSURANCE BUILDING AND CAREW TOWER IN BACKGROUND.

Schiffer Publishing Ltd

4880 Lower Valley Road, Atglen, PA 19310 USA

Other Schiffer Books by Mary L. Martin
Bathing Beauties of the Roaring '20s. Mary L. Martin & Tina Skinner.
Greetings from New Orleans: A History in Postcards. Mary L. Martin, Tina Skinner
Hawaiian Fish. Mary L. Martin
Hollywood Homes: Postcard Views of Early Stars' Estates. Mary L. Martin, Tina Skinner, & Tammy Ward
Miami Memories: A Midcentury Journey. Mary L. Martin, Tina Skinner, & Nathaniel Wolfgang-Price
Midget Exhibit: Images from the Heyday of Dwarf Display. Mary L. Martin & Tina Skinner
Naughty Victorians and Edwardians: Early Images of Bathing Beauties. Mary L. Martin & Tina Skinner
Cape Cod Memories: An Illustrated History in Postcards. Karen Choppa & Mary L. Martin
Geisha Women of Japan's Flower & Willow World. Tina Skinner, Mary L. Martin, & Wes Ponder
Greetings from Havre de Grace. Craig David & Mary L. Martin
Hawaii Remembered: Postcards from Paradise. Tina Skinner, Mary L. Martin, & Nathanial Wolfgang-Price
Historic Christmas Art: Santas, Angels, Poinsettia, Holly, Nativity, Children, and More Royalty-free Images on CD. Mary L. Martin & Tina Skinner
Historic Holiday Art: New Year, Valentines, St. Patrick's Day, Easter, July 4th, Halloween, & Thanksgiving. Tina Skinner & Mary L. Martin
Lighthouse Views. Tina Skinner, Mary Martin Postcards
Memories of Memphis: A History in Postcards. Ginny Parfitt & Mary L. Martin

Other Schiffer Books on Related Subjects
Advertising Postcards. Robert Reed
Art Deco Architecture: Miami Beach Poscards. Paul Clemence
Birds of Cape Cod & the Islands in Postcards. Roger S. Everett
Cape May Postcards.
Card Photographs: A Guide to Their History and Value. Lou W. McCulloch
Greetings from Ohio: Vintage Postcards 1900-1960s. Robert Reed.
Miami Beach Postcards.
Mies van der Rohe's Farnsworth House Postcard Book. Paul Clemence
Newport News: A Vintage Postcard Tour. Harold Cones & John Bryant

Copyright © 2007 by Mary L. Martin
Library of Congress Control Number: 2006928512

Designed by Mark David Bowyer
Type set in Americana XBd BT / Zurich BT

ISBN: 0-7643-2561-2
Printed in China
1 2 3 4

Published by Schiffer Publishing Ltd.
4880 Lower Valley Road
Atglen, PA 19310
Phone: (610) 593-1777; Fax: (610) 593-2002
E-mail: Info@schifferbooks.com

For the largest selection of fine reference books on this and related subjects, please visit our web site at **www.schifferbooks.com**
We are always looking for people to write books on new and related subjects. If you have an idea for a book please contact us at the above address.

This book may be purchased from the publisher.
Include $3.95 for shipping.
Please try your bookstore first.
You may write for a free catalog.

In Europe, Schiffer books are distributed by
Bushwood Books
6 Marksbury Ave.
Kew Gardens
Surrey TW9 4JF England
Phone: 44 (0) 20 8392-8585; Fax: 44 (0) 20 8392-9876
E-mail: info@bushwoodbooks.co.uk
Website: www.bushwoodbooks.co.uk
Free postage in the U.K., Europe; air mail at cost.

Contents

Historic Images Through Postcards

Postcards are said to be the most popular collectible history has ever known. The urge to horde them sprang up with the birth of this means of communication at the turn of the twentieth century, and has endured great changes in the printing industry. Today, postcard shows take place every weekend somewhere in the country, or the world, and millions of pieces of ephemera lie in wait for those who collect obscure topics or town views.

Postcards once served as the email of their day. They were the fastest, most popular means of communication beginning in the 1890s in the United States. These timely cards provided a way to send visual scenes through the mail along with brief messages– a way to enchant friends and family with the places travelers visited, to send local scenes, or to share favorite topics of imagery. They even provided the latest breaking news, as images of fires, floods, shipwrecks, and festivals were often available in postcard form within hours of an event. Moreover, mail delivery was received by most homes in the United States at least twice a day. So someone might send a morning postcard inviting a friend to dinner that evening, and receive an RSVP in time to shop for food.

The messages shared and the beautiful scenes combine to create the timeless appeal of postcards as a collectible. Most importantly, history is recorded by the pictures of the times, moments in time reflecting an alluring past.

Dating Postcards

Pioneer Era (1893-1898): Most pioneer cards in today's collections begin with cards placed on sale at the Columbian Exposition in Chicago on May 1, 1893. These were illustrations on government printed postal cards and privately printed souvenir cards. The government cards had the printed one-cent stamp, while souvenir cards required a two-cent adhesive postage stamp to be applied. Writing was not permitted on the address side of the card.

Private Mailing Card Era (1898-1901): On May 19, 1898, private printers were granted permission, by an act of Congress, to print and sell cards that bore the inscription "Private Mailing Card." A one-cent adhesive stamp was required. A dozen or more American printers began to take postcards seriously. Writing was still not permitted on the back.

Post Card Era - Undivided Back (1901-1907): New U.S. postal regulations on December 24, 1901, stipulated that the words "Post Card" should be printed at the top of the address side of privately printed cards. Government-issued cards were to be designated as "Postal Cards." Writing was still not permitted on the address side. In this era, private citizens began to take black and white photographs and have them printed on paper with post card backs.

Early Divided Back Era (1907-1914): Postcards with a divided back were permitted in Britain in 1902, but not in the U.S. until March 1, 1907. The address was to be written on the right side; the left side was for writing messages. Many millions of cards were published in this era. Up to this point, most postcards were printed in Germany, which was far ahead of the United States in the use of lithographic processes. With the advent of World War I, the supply of postcards for American consumption switched from Germany to England and the United States.

White Border Era (1915-1930): Most United States postcards were printed during this period. To save ink, publishers left a clear border around the view, thus these postcards are referred to as "White Border" cards. The relatively high cost of labor, along with inexperience and changes in public taste, resulted in the production of poor quality cards during this period. Furthermore, strong competition in a narrowing market caused many publishers to go out of business.

Linen Era (1930-1944): New printing processes allowed printing on postcards with high rag content that created a textured finish. These cheap cards allowed the use of gaudy dyes for coloring.

Photochrome Era (1945 to date): "Chrome" postcards began to dominate the scene soon after the Union Oil Company placed them in its western service stations in 1939. Mike Roberts pioneered with his "WESCO" cards soon after World War II. Three-dimensional postcards also appeared in this era.

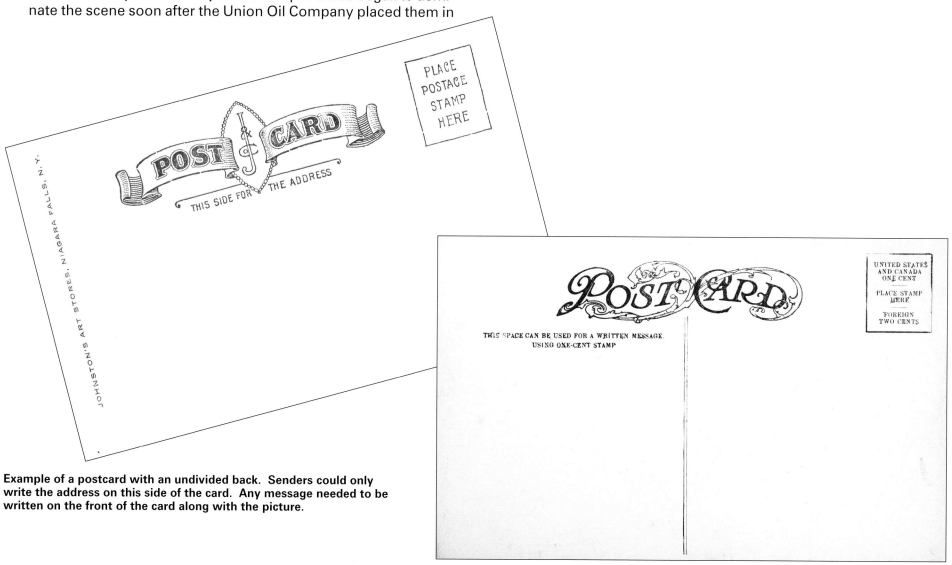

Example of a postcard with an undivided back. Senders could only write the address on this side of the card. Any message needed to be written on the front of the card along with the picture.

Sample of a postcard with a divided back. Senders were allowed to put an address on the right hand side of the postcard and a message on the left side.

Introduction

The dynamic city of Cincinnati, located on the north bank of the Ohio River, is the perfect place to study the growth of an American town and its development into a thriving metropolis. In the course of this natural form of historic time stamping, individuals communicated with one another in a way that spoke of visual journeys that lined the past with a reality caught in a split second of time—the postcard. See clearly the magnificent Cincinnati lifestyles of old, rich with architectural wonder and history, changing through the decades, and upgraded and polished to meet the needs of the day. Note the waterways, shining with an allure of financial security, once housing hardworking (and sometimes romantic) steamers—first as a means of prosperity and then expanded to entertainment pursuits as time moved forward. See the rails and trails of progress; the introduction of education and religion; the arm of politics and law; the trends in commerce and in relaxation. And, of course, witness the view of both city and suburban landscapes that never fail to offer the grace and solitude of quiet pride for a city understanding the importance of art and culture. Whether daily life or business strife, Cincinnati was the place to be as it made its bright mark on history.

Bird's-Eye from Mt. Adams, Cincinnati, Ohio.

Bird's-eye view from Mt. Adams, Cincinnati, Ohio. This famous Cincinnati hill was named after President John Quincy Adams. In the early 1800s, great success in cultivating grapes by the hill's owner, Nicholas Longworth, made Mt. Adams (for a short period of time) the wine-making center of America.

Cancelled 1917, $6-8

With many nicknames—"The Queen City," "The Queen of the West," "The Blue Chip City," or even abbreviated to "Cincy" or "The Nati"—Cincinnati blends the best of European style with an equal southern charm that drew both travelers and tourists to the town throughout United States history. Still another name, "City of Seven Hills," is thought to be a nickname that came from an idealistic reference to Rome, but there is no real consensus regarding *which* hills are the specific hills in the name.

In the heart of the city, historic Fountain Square overlooks a bustling main street that presents historic hotels and business buildings that have changed into world-class establishments through the years.

At the same time, the slow, lazy Ohio River provides a beautiful atmosphere for many who seek a thought-provoking way of life. Regardless, there is something in Cincinnati that has drawn masses to its splendor.

Of course, as a popular means of communication, postcards traveled from this "Queen City" to those around the world who would enjoy the images and messages of the time. Those images of *that* moment in *that* time so long ago are the same images you will see in this pictorial journey. Showing postcards throughout the early to mid twentieth century, *Greetings from Cincinnati* will tell the story of a city ready to be explored and revisited. Enjoy the trip!

The Cincinnati skyline from Kentucky.

Circa 1907, $ 4-6

"Greetings from Cincinnati, Ohio"

Cancelled 1951, $4-6

A Brief Historical Overview

What's In A Name?

Cincinnati was not always the name of this historic town in Ohio. John Filson, a Kentucky pioneer, surveyor, teacher, and author of the time, named the town "Losantiville"—meaning *the city opposite the mouth of the Licking River*. (Though Filson wrote *Discovery, Settlement, and Present State of Kentucky* in 1784, he is perhaps known best for the popular, "Adventures of Colonel Daniel Boon," which is allegedly Boone's autobiography.) Losantiville, however, was not a safe place to be in the late 1700s. The local Indian population was not inclined to give up their heritage and territory without conflict. It was during such a clash that Filson mysteriously disappeared and was not heard from again.

Another account (in 1788), however, credits three different prominent Kentuckians—Colonel Robert Patterson, Israel Ludlow, and Matthias Denman—for the town's name of Losantiville. The three men purchased eight hundred acres along the Ohio River at the mouth of the Licking River, and each held a specific component of the overall plan to build a city at this site. Denman was responsible for securing the money needed for the sale. Patterson found the people to settle the land by advertising for settlers in Kentucky. Ludlow surveyed the land for the proper layout of the city. (It has also been said that the mysteriously missing Filson, mentioned earlier, was the man who surveyed the land—and not Ludlow.)

In 1789, the land was parceled out in half-acre and four-acre lot sizes. The smaller lots were situated near the city's center with outlying land reserved for larger lots. Land was granted using a lottery system, with the first thirty settlers receiving two free lots, one of each type.

Arthur St. Clair, who was Governor of the Northwest Territory of the United States at that time, did not like the town's name. He made the decision, in 1790, to change it to its current name, in honor of the Society of the Cincinnati—a group of patriots who honored General George Washington. George Washington was considered a latter-day Cincinnatus—a Roman general of the same name who saved his city during a time of conflict. Patriotism was an important attribute of the time in Cincinnati. In fact, there were so many patriots in Cincinnati during the Revolutionary War, that, to this day, one can find a larger than normal number of descendants deriving from soldiers who were granted land in Ohio.

A historic scene in Burnet Woods Park. Now adjoining the University of Cincinnati at Clifton Avenue between Martin Luther King Jr. Drive and Ludlow, the development of Burnet Woods Park was first considered by Robert W. Burnet and William S. Groesbeck in 1871.

Cancelled 1910, $ 5-7

Driveway in Burnet Woods Park, Cincinnati, O.

As the city thrived, the practice of naming Cincinnati was not over. Nicknames continued to flourish. In 1819, Henry Wadsworth Longfellow called Cincinnati the "Queen of the West" in a local newspaper because it was a very important stop for the Underground Railroad, helping slaves escape to the north. The Underground Railroad offered a system of safe hiding places for runaway slaves, and Cincinnati residents acted as "conductors" and guides in an effort to make sure that the slaves were sent unharmed to welcoming areas.

Then in the early 1800s, the meatpacking industry brought still more name notoriety. Farmers routinely brought livestock to Cincinnati to be slaughtered, processed, and sold to buyers from other parts of the country. Thus, the metropolis was dubbed "Porkopolis" around 1835, as it became the country's chief hog packing center. Herds of pigs traveled the streets.

Come One, Come All!

As Governor St. Clair and other military officials planned campaigns against the Native Americans—who were actively fighting for their land and rights during 1790 and 1791— thousands of militiamen from Pennsylvania and Kentucky flooded the new city. Still later, despite St. Clair's defeat at the hands of the Indians, settlers descended upon Cincinnati to make their fortunes in business along the Ohio River. (Because of its strategic location on the Ohio River, steam navigation made an impact on commerce that would grow the city to 115,000 people by 1850.)

By 1792, the settlers erected profitable warehouses in Cincinnati to provide supplies to both soldiers and people traveling along the river. In 1794, still more settlers arrived as General Anthony Wayne waged a successful expedition against the Indians at the Battle of Fallen Timbers. Business was thriving in "Cincy."

Though Cincinnati was chartered in 1802 as a village, it wasn't long before it was incorporated as a city. By 1803, the year that the United States Army abandoned Fort Washington (built in 1789 to protect early settlements), the city had roughly one thousand inhabitants. Big business was growing Cincinnati's population beyond village status as 1819 arrived and departed. The city continued to grow, reaching nearly ten thousand residents by 1820.

Covington, Kentucky, riverfront looking from the Marmet Coal Yards in Cincinnati.

Circa 1907, $5-7

Workers beneath the Cincinnati and Newport Bridge.

Circa 1907, $4-6

Business and Industry in Cincinnati

The River

Cincinnati continued to grow during the nineteenth century, mainly because the Ohio River gave residents fantastic business opportunities. With so much river travel, people working and visiting Cincinnati needed places to stay, food to eat, and taverns to drown their aches and pains after their hard-working days. Steamboats were built and repaired; farmers brought their crops to sell or ship down the Ohio and Mississippi Rivers to New Orleans, Louisiana, and beyond; warehouse workers loaded and unloaded supplies. Steamers provided a much easier and nicer ride for the workers of Cincinnati, in the early to mid 1800s, because it was more difficult for the angry Native Americans to attack the steamboats than other modes of transportation available. The city prospered.

This particular steamboat landing was located adjacent to a railyard, making it very convenient for shippers to move their products by both land and sea.

Circa 1907, $5-7

Steamers provided the workers of Cincinnati a way to ship their goods across the Ohio River. The first steamboat docked in Cincinnati in 1811.

Circa 1914, $5-7

Scene on the Ohio River at Cincinnati, Ohio.

A closeup of a working riverboat scene on the Ohio River displays docking practices.

Circa 1914, $ 5-7

Steamer Entering Locks Fern Bank Dam, Ohio River, Cincinnati, Ohio.

A working steamer enters the locks of Fern Bank Dam. The dam was constructed in 1911. Much later, in 1963, a new group of nineteen dams were built, and the level of water was raised to twenty-five feet, allowing larger ships to pass through.

Circa 1914, $3-5

11

It didn't take long for the fine folk of Cincinnati to realize that, in addition to transportation and business concerns, the Ohio River could provide them with still another important pastime and high-yield commercial venue. Recreational steamers became not only a way to relax and enjoy what life had to offer, but also became an additional profit-maker for the city.

Steamers were a popular venue for postcards. They provided an exciting message to send to varied parts of the world: *Cincinnati is a fun place to be*. An underlying message may have been: *Don't you wish* you *were here?*

The Island Queen lands at Coney Island, Cincinnati, Ohio 40

Steamer Island Queen, Cincinnati. O.

Coney Island was no stranger to recreational river boating. The *Island Queen*, shown here, took passengers for a twenty-mile round-trip voyage along the Ohio River between Broadway and Coney Island. The big all-steel, glass-enclosed steamer had a capacity of 4,000 people.

Circa 1930s, $ 3-5

Traveling on the *Island Queen* at night was a special treat for passengers who enjoyed looking at the slow and lazy waters of the Ohio River from the comfort of this luxury steamer.

Circa early 1900s, $4-6

SKY LINE FROM THE OHIO RIVER, CINCINNATI, OHIO.

A popular scene for Cincinnati postcards—the skyline looking from across the Ohio River.

Cancelled 1928, $ 4-6

Cincinnati, O. Mt. Adams – View from the River.

Though the *Island Queen* was a wonderful touring boat, people aboard were still cognizant of life in a riverboat town as they passed by loading and shipping docks.

Circa 1907, $4-6

13

The Rails

The riverboats were not to be the only mode of transportation that affected Cincinnati business and commerce. In the early 1800s, the need for railroads became evident. This mode offered benefits in two different practical categories. Not only could businesses without access to the canals and waterways ship products to areas around the country, but residents would also have connections to other areas of the state not available earlier. Rail travel was also a comparatively cheap way of traveling and for shipping products. The river had competition.

CINCINNATI UNION TERMINAL AT NIGHT, CINCINNATI, OHIO   3A-H934

At night, the Union Terminal offered a grand fountain display. Over 200 trains per day—108 into the station and 108 out of the station—ran through the terminal in its heyday.

Circa 1930s, $6-8

CINCINNATI UNION TERMINAL, CINCINNATI, OHIO   3A-H296

A museum today, the Art Deco-style Union Terminal was constructed between 1929 and 1933 to serve the rail needs of the area.

Circa 1930s, $ 6-8

18—Lobby, Union Terminal, Cincinnati, Ohio

3A-H933

Winold Reise designed and created a color mosaic mural for the rotunda at the Union Terminal, two murals for the baggage area, two for the departing and arriving train boards, and fourteen smaller murals depicting local industry. The industries represented were: piano making, radio broadcasting, roof manufacturing, tanning, airplane and parts manufacturing, ink making, laundry-machinery manufacturing, meat packing, drug and chemical manufacturing, printing and publishing, foundry products operations, sheet steel making, soap making, and machine tools manufacturing.

Cancelled 1944, $ 7-9

14—Concourse, Union Terminal, Cincinnati, Ohio

3A-H932

Reise spent about two years in the creation and design of the varied murals. Note on this postcard the concourse of Union Terminal and the large world map located at the rear. This beautiful design was another of Reise's mural creations. The murals were moved to the Cincinnati/Northern Kentucky International Airport in 1974 in an effort to preserve them.

Cancelled 1943, $ 7-9

7—Bird's-Eye View of Cincinnati, Ohio, Union Terminal in Foreground

3A-H931

A bird's-eye view of Cininnati with the Union Terminal in the foreground. Union Terminal, in the present day, serves as a high-end shopping mall.

Cancelled 1944, $ 6-8

The Pennsylvania and L. & N. Railroad Station in Cincinnati.

Cancelled 1911, $ 8-10

PENNSYLVANIA AND L.&N. RAILROAD STATION.
CINCINNATI, O.

Central Union Station, Cincinnati, Ohio, No. 68.

Central Union Station, No. 68.

Circa 1907, $ 8-10

Street Cars to Buses

Streetcars provided another important method of transportation. They were constructed to allow easier travel to Kentucky and back for Cincinnatians. Streetcar routes went through an elimination process in the 1930s, with buses replacing the cars.

Dixie Terminal Building, Cincinnati, Ohio.

The Dixie Terminal Building was opened for streetcar use in 1921 to allow easier transportation between Kentucky and Cincinnati. Streetcars were still another way to increase efficient people movement. Inside the building, a large picture window looks out to the nearby Roebling Suspension Bridge. Later, the Dixie Terminal was changed into a bus terminal.

Cancelled 1924, $ 6-8

The Bridges

By the mid-1800s, it was obvious that transportation concerns for Cincinnati would include the need for bridges to connect the city to nearby Kentucky. There were issues relating to the specifications of the first bridge—i.e., the piers could not obstruct the shipping of goods by the river and the bridge needed to be high enough to accommodate the high stacks of the steamers that would pass beneath. However, construction was started in 1856 with eased restrictions. (The length was reduced to 1,000 feet and the height was reduced to 100 feet.)

11468 SUSPENSION BRIDGE, CINCINNATI, OHIO.

The Covington and Cincinnati Bridge was officially named the John A. Roebling Bridge in the 1980s; but local citizens have called it simply "The Suspension Bridge" since 1866 when it was first built. When the bridge first opened, a horse and buggy driver would pay a toll of fifteen cents to cross. If there were three horses rather than one, and a carriage was being pulled, the toll was twenty-five cents. Walkers were charged a penny.

Circa 1914, $ 5-7

Bridge construction continued for over ten years, but financial shortages and the Civil War slowed completion of the bridge until December of 1866. The bridge, known as the John A. Roebling Bridge, was a prototype for the design of the famed Brooklyn Bridge in New York.

Because Cincinnati was located along the Ohio River, four bridges were erected to connect Newport and Covington, Kentucky, to Cincinnati. In addition to the John A. Roebling Suspension Bridge, the Daniel Carter Beard Bridge and the Purple People Bridge (a pedestrian-only bridge), along with other varied viaducts, have also become special landmarks.

The Suspension Bridge, viewing Cincinnati from Covingon, Kentucky. The bridge was the world's longest in 1866 and the first to use both vertical suspenders and diagonal stays fanning from either tower.

Cancelled 1947, $ 4-6

Today, The Suspension Bridge continues to be of paramount importance to Cincinnati. Remaining an important crossing for traffic, its magnificance and beauty will always be more than decoration.

Circa 1907, $ 5-7

Another view of Cincinnati from Covington, Kentucky.

Cancelled 1932, $ 4-6

A view looking from the Kentucky side of the Ohio River into Cincinnati.

Cancelled 1914, $4-6

Cincinnati, O. - C. and O. Ry. Bridge - View from Kentucky Side, Ohio River.

A view of the Ohio River and the four bridges of Cincinnati. The city of Cincinnati is the second largest city in Ohio and the metropolis of the southern part of the State.

Cancelled 1942, $ 5-7

Ohio River and The Four Bridges, Cincinnati, Ohio

34

Marsh Studio

Bird's-eye View of Cincinnati, Ohio, showing Ohio River, L. & N. Bridge and Southern R. R. Bridge.

A view of Cincinnati showing the Ohio River, L. & N. Bridge, and the Southern Railroad Bridge. In 1872 the first Ohio River railroad crossing was built and named the L. & N. Bridge. The Southern Railroad Bridge connects the western part of Cincinnati to Ludlow, Kentucky. The bridge opened in 1877 and is still the busiest in the city.

Cancelled 1913, $ 6-8

Harrison Ave. Viaduct, West End, Cincinnati, O.

Viaducts, too, were part of the transportation plans in Cincinnati. The Harrison Avenue Viaduct was the first vehicular viaduct in the Cincinnati area, standing to the northwest of the city from 1908 until the opening of the Western Hills Viaduct in 1932. It did not follow the path of Harrison Avenue, however, and the street remained open along its original course until 1932.

Circa 1907, $ 5-7

The Eighth Street Viaduct was built in 1910, with a twenty-foot-wide deck, similar in appearance to the Harrison Avenue Viaduct.

Cancelled 1913, $ 5-7

EIGHTH STREET V

Hopple Street Viaduct, Cincinnati, Ohio.

THE CINCINNATI UNION STOCK YARD CO.

The Hopple Street Viaduct, built in 1914 with a forty-foot, four-lane deck, was situated northwest of downtown Cincinnati, connecting the Mill Creek and the very big Queensgate Railroad Yard.

Circa 1914, $ 5-7

LOUISVIL

The Buildings and Streets of Cincinnati

As the city became a hub for riverboats and rail traffic, the buildings and streets of Cincinnati developed into a town—filled with the necessities of living that complimented commerce. Buildings of quiet magnificence surrounded the historic Fountain Square, located in the heart of the downtown area. Buildings, hotels, churches, educational facilities, hospitals, scenic landscapes, and attractions all marked the charm and excitement of a growing city and added to the everyday lifestyles of city residents.

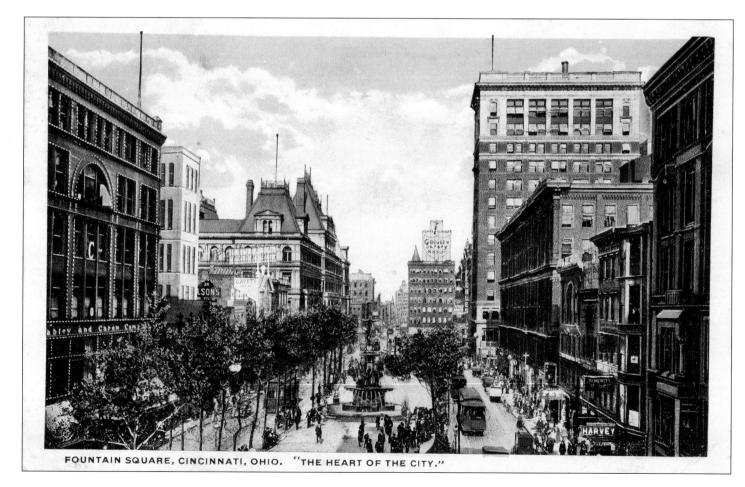

FOUNTAIN SQUARE, CINCINNATI, OHIO. "THE HEART OF THE CITY."

The famous landmark, Fountain Square, is called, "The Heart of the City." Located at Fifth and Vine amidst a landscape constructed with cement (a hardscape), Fountain Square was (and is today) the centerpiece for area business, culture, and tourism. In the center of this busy square is the bronze Tyler Davidson Fountain, donated to the city by well-known resident, Henry Probasco, and dedicated in 1871 to his brother-in-law, Tyler Davidson.

Cancelled 1920, $6-8

FOUNTAIN SQUARE, CINCINNATI, OHIO.

Because Fountain Square is surrounded by excellent business opportunities, shopping, hotels, and restaurants have filled the area to meet the needs of workers and visitors.

Circa 1914, $ 6-8

THE ESPLANADE, FOUNTAIN SQUARE, CINCINNATI, OHIO.

Fountain Square has been proclaimed one of the best-known and most-visited street areas in Cincinnati.

Cancelled 1919, $ 6-8

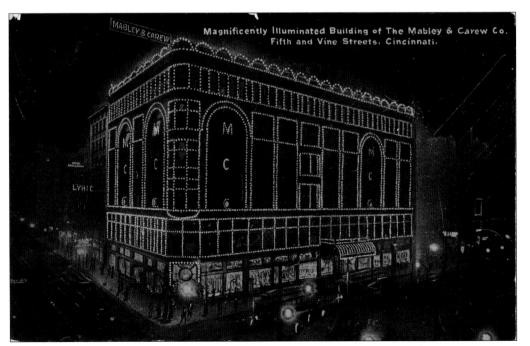

The Mabley and Carew Department Store was located at Fifth and Vine, but was eventually torn down in the 1980s to make way for Fountain Square West. Fountain Square West was intended to be the new tallest building in Cincinnati. This new building was never erected—but may be in future plans for the city.

Circa 1907, $4-6

24

Some DAY you will BE A MEMBER OF THIS — UNCLE GUS — 2/18/07

PUP.. BY ILL.. POST. CARD CO.. NEW YORK.

870   Chamber of Commerce, Cincinnati, O.

CAREW TOWER
CINCINNATI, O.

In 1839, seventy-six businesses and individuals brought local businessmen together at a meeting at the Young Men's Mercantile Library Association headquarters at Fourth and Walnut (in the old Cincinnati College Building). The discussion delved into uniform regulations and a unison action in the promotion of mutual interests. This, then, was the birth of The Cincinnati Chamber of Commerce. This photo postcard shows the Chamber's building that was constructed in 1889 and destroyed by fire in 1911.

Cancelled 1907, $ 5-7

The Carew Tower, fully constructed in 1930, was the tallest building in Cincinnati—49 stories tall (some postcards portray the building as 48 stories tall) and 574 feet above street level. Overlooking the Ohio River, this building is a National Historic Landmark. Within the lobby of the hotel, you will now find a restaurant—Palm Court—that is described as having the "finest example of French Art Deco architecture in the world." Art deco themes can be seen in many areas of the building and especially in the grillwork of the elevators and lights.

Circa 1907, $4-6

4—Fountain Square and Carew Tower at Night, Cincinnati, Ohio

Construction for the Carew Tower began in 1929, just prior to the great Stock Market crash. Because the crash greatly affected the budget for completing the building, the amount of decorative metalwork was lessened and there was a change from limestone to brick cladding.

Circa 1930s, $ 3-5

Ingall's Building, Largest Concrete Building in the World. Cincinnati, O.

The Ingalls
Building was built in 1903,
and was the world's first reinforced
concrete structure, sporting sixteen stories.
At the time of construction, there were many skeptics, but the success of the building gave way to acceptance for concrete construction for high rises in the United States. It was designated a National Historic Civil Engineering Landmark in 1974, and in 1975 it was added to the National Register of Historic Places.

Circa 1907, $ 4-6

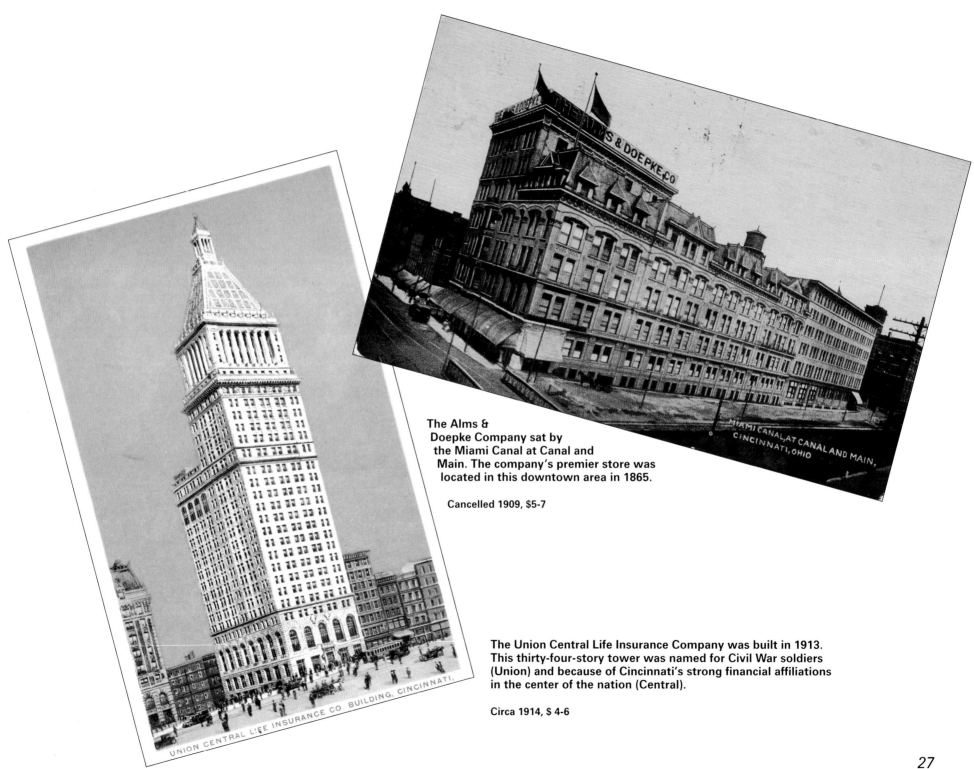

The Alms &
Doepke Company sat by
the Miami Canal at Canal and
Main. The company's premier store was
located in this downtown area in 1865.

Cancelled 1909, $5-7

The Union Central Life Insurance Company was built in 1913.
This thirty-four-story tower was named for Civil War soldiers
(Union) and because of Cincinnati's strong financial affiliations
in the center of the nation (Central).

Circa 1914, $ 4-6

FIRST NATIONAL BANK, CINCINNATI, OHIO.

The First National Bank in Cincinnati was another example of a tall skyscraper.

Cancelled 1909, $4-6

Union Trust Building, Cincinnati, Ohio.

67003

The Union Trust Building in Cincinnati.

Circa 1907, $4-6

28

The Provident Savings Bank and Trust Company in Cincinnati.

Circa 1930s, $3-5

The Merchants Building
on Sixth Avenue, bordering
College, in Cincinnati.

Cancelled 1916, $4-6

TRACTION BUILDING.
CINCINNATI,
OHIO.

Hand Colored.

THE ALTENHEIM, CINCINNATI, O.

The Traction Building, a high-rise office complex.

Circa 1907, $4-6

The Altenheim—a German Old Men's and Widow's Home—in Cincinnati is an assisted-living resource that is supported by local humanitarians.

Circa early 1900s, $4-6

BUSINESS MEN'S CLUB, NINTH & RACE STS., CINCINNATI, O.

The Business Men's Club was an organization of local businessmen, similar to the Chamber of Commerce, with varied interests and projects considered for group participation. One such project came about as Mayor Henry Hunt, in 1912, appointed a Commission to consider avenues available to secure high-speed electric railway services. The Commission asked the Commercial Association, the Business Men's Club, and the Chamber of Commerce to come together in a funding effort. Over ten thousand dollars was raised towards the project.

Cancelled 1912, $ 5-7

In 1856, the YMCA in Cincinnati offered the first known *English as a Second Language* course for German immigrants.

Circa 1914, $5-7

Young Men's Christian Association, Cincinnati, Ohio.

Glovernook, Home for the Blind, Mt. Healthy near Cincinnati, Ohio, Formerly the Home of Alice and Phoebe Cary.

Max Weil & Co. Cincinnati, No. 20.

Though the postcard shows this building's name as *Glovernook,* the actual name is *Clovernook,* and was the childhood home of Alice and Phoebe Cary. Following the deaths of the Cary women, their home was preserved as a home for blind women. In the early 1900s, the "Cary Cottage" became the first home for the blind in the state, its mission to assist women with visual impairments, help with their employment, and aid with the provision of a home for them. Today, the facility services both men and women, providing a skilled staff to support the revised mission.

Circa early 1900s, $4-6

Chester Park—named after a popular race-horse, Lady Chester—was the headquarters for the Queen City Jockey Club in the 1870s. Later, in the 1890s, the park became an amusement facility that held bicycle outings and races.

Cancelled 1908, $ 4-6

CLUB-HOUSE CHESTER PARK CINCINNATI, O.

Country Club.   23. - CINCINNATI (Ohio).
Handcolored

The Country Club in Cincinnati.

Circa early 1900s, $4-6

ODD FELLOWS TEMPLE, CINCINNATI, OHIO   14

The Odd Fellow Temple is a sandstone structure that was built in 1870. The Independent Order of Odd Fellows is an organization—both charitable and compassionate—that reaches out to improve the lives of good people. They visit the sick, aid the troubled, educate orphans, and bury the dead.

Cancelled 1925, $ 4-6

33

Government

Like many cities in the United States, Cincinnati began with an informal expression of government. In fact, in the late nineteenth century and moving into the early twentieth century, politics and related decisions were oftentimes made in the company of tavern and saloonkeepers. But in the 1920s, reform stormed the city, demanding that the government become reputable and a municipal model for the entire nation.

This change in political climate was of paramount importance because not only had corruption been evident in government, but the city was nearly bankrupt and lacking the means to even protect itself from fire and other abuses. A charter, in 1924, eliminated the old political structure, and Cincinnatians voted in a package that was more amenable to the health and welfare of the city.

Some of the government and public buildings are depicted on the following pages.

Government Square showing the bustling activity of a growing city and government.

Cancelled 1916, $6-8

Court House, Main & Court Sts.   Cincinnati, O.

The Courthouse in Cincinnati has had a colorful history. The first courthouse, built in 1802, was lost by fire in 1814 due to carelessness by soldiers stationed there. The second courthouse, built on the same site, burned down in 1884—this time by an angry mob protesting a murder trial involving black and white racial discrimination.

Cancelled 1906, $4-6

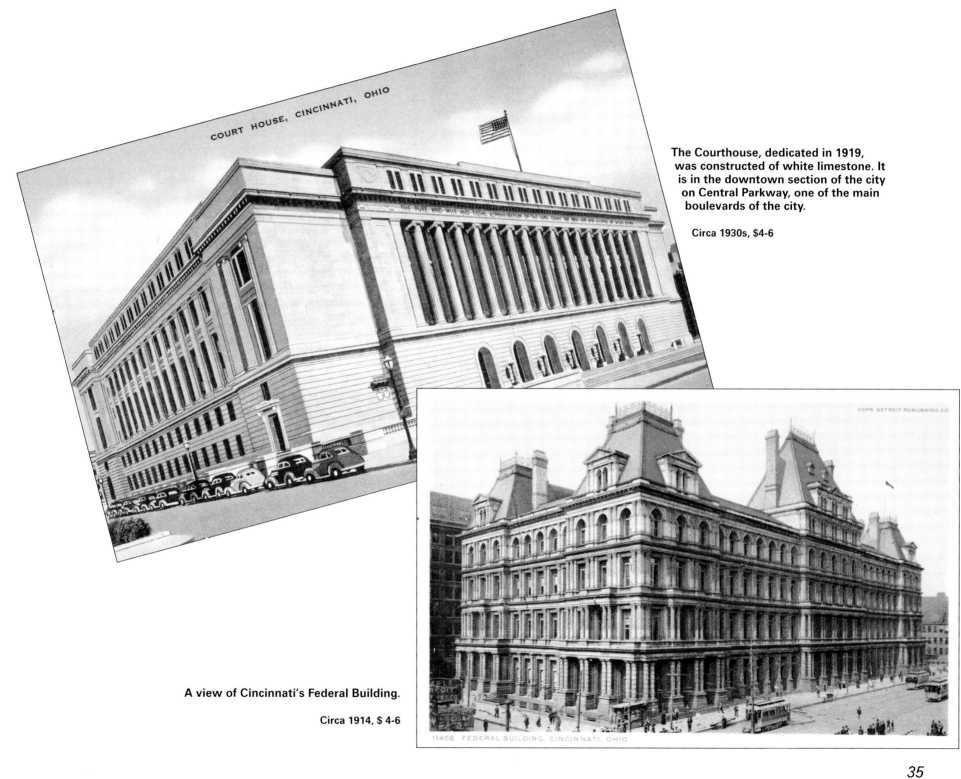

COURT HOUSE, CINCINNATI, OHIO

THE PURE AND WISE AND EQUAL ADMINISTRATION OF LAWS FORMS THE FIRST END AND BLESSING OF SOCIAL UNION

The Courthouse, dedicated in 1919, was constructed of white limestone. It is in the downtown section of the city on Central Parkway, one of the main boulevards of the city.

Circa 1930s, $4-6

A view of Cincinnati's Federal Building.

Circa 1914, $ 4-6

11458 FEDERAL BUILDING, CINCINNATI, OHIO

COPR. DETROIT PUBLISHING CO.

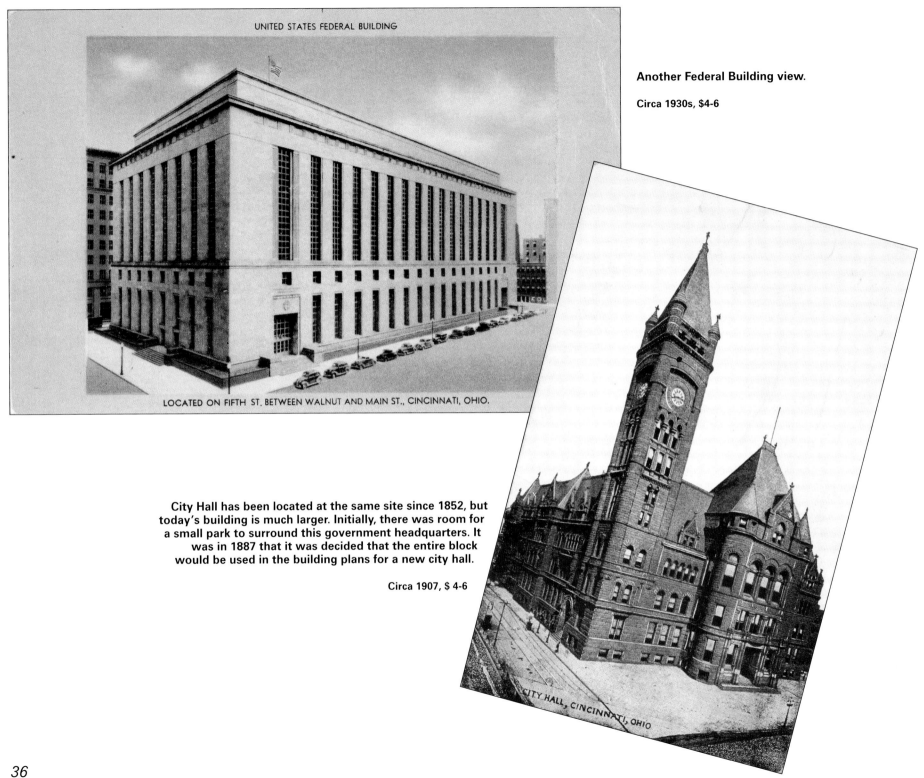

UNITED STATES FEDERAL BUILDING

LOCATED ON FIFTH ST. BETWEEN WALNUT AND MAIN ST., CINCINNATI, OHIO.

Another Federal Building view.

Circa 1930s, $4-6

City Hall has been located at the same site since 1852, but today's building is much larger. Initially, there was room for a small park to surround this government headquarters. It was in 1887 that it was decided that the entire block would be used in the building plans for a new city hall.

Circa 1907, $ 4-6

CITY HALL, CINCINNATI, OHIO

Cincinnati, O. City Hall.

The Cincinnati United States Post Office.

Circa 1907, $4-6

Again in the mid-1900s, proposals for a new City Hall were offered. However, at that time, the public tendency leaned toward the preservation of historic buildings rather than building new.

Circa 1907, $4-6

Post Office, Cincinnati, Ohio.

Another view of the United States Post Office in Cincinnati.

Cancelled 1911, $ 4-6

WORK HOUSE, CINCINNATI.

The original Cincinnati Workhouse was operated in Hamilton County from 1867 to 1869, with the building entirely completed in 1870. Convicts in the Workhouse produced products (i.e. shoes, castings) for manufacturers. The Workhouse operated into the twentieth century.

Cancelled 1907, $ 3-5

PUBLIC LIBRARY, CINCINNATI, OHIO.

The Grand Army of the Republic Memorial Building in Cincinnati. G.A.R. was originally established in Indianapolis in 1866 by Union veterans.

Cancelled 1916, $ 4-6

It was in 1802 that the first series of libraries were introduced to Cincinnati, but locations were inadequate for public needs until 1870. At that time, the Cincinnati Library moved into the building at Eighth and Vine.

Circa 1914, $4-6

Educational Institutions

Education, of course, has always been an important part of Cincinnati life, as was the case across the nation. Nathaniel Guilford, in 1829, was responsible for having a law passed that would end private monopolies in schools. This was the birth of a public school system.

The city housed not only public schools, but also a variety of private and religion-based schools. In addition, the city boasted of fine colleges and universities that have continued to be a vital component of the city's sustained growth.

The 16th District School in the Mt. Auburn area of Cincinnati.

Circa 1907, $4-6

The New Hughes High School opened in 1910. Located at Clifton and McMillan Avenues in Clifton Heights, the building had nearly five acres of floor space and a 145-foot tower over its arched entrance.

Circa 1907, $5-7

East Side High School, Cincinnati, Ohio.

Eastside High School is now known as Withrow High School.

Cancelled 1925, $ 5-7

New Woodward High School, Cincinnati, O.

New Woodward High School, founded by William Woodward, began in 1831 as a four-room, redbrick schoolhouse. Mr. Woodward's thinking since 1819 had been that there needed to be some provision for education for those who could not afford it.

Cancelled 1909, $ 5-7

Avondale High School, Cincinnati, Ohio.

Avondale High School in Cincinnati.

Cancelled 1912, $ 5-7

Clifton Public School,
Clifton Ave. Cincinnati, O.

Clifton Public School on Clifton Avenue in Cincinnati.

Cancelled 1912, $ 5-7

The St. Francis School at Liberty and Vine Streets in Cincinnati.

Cancelled 1911, $ 4-6

ST. FRANCIS SCHOOL, LIBERTY AND VINE STREETS, CINCINNATI, O.

43

Harriett Beecher Stowe School, Cincinnati, Ohio

42

The Harriet Beecher Stowe School in Cincinnati. This Junior High and Elementary School was founded by Dr. Jennie D. Porter and erected in 1923. (Harriet Beecher Stowe was the daughter of Presbyterian minister Lyman Beecher, the influential slavery abolitionist. Harriet wrote the famed novel *Uncle Tom's Cabin* about the experiences she had at the cabin as a young woman.)

Circa 1930s, $ 4-6

Ohio Mechanics Institute, Cincinnati.

One of the first technical schools in the nation, the Ohio Mechanics Institute provided practical training for mechanics in Cincinnati. Not only were there organized lectures, but also a large library and reading room were part of the school's success. By the 1850s, about twelve hundred members attended at a cost of three dollars each for membership.

Cancelled 1909, $ 5-7

3341 a. Art School. Eden Park, Cincinnati, O.

Recognized as the McMicken School of Art and Design in 1869, it was suggested that the school be moved to an Eden Park location when the Cincinnati Museum was established there in 1885.

Circa early 1900s, $ 5-7

Art School and Art Museum, (Eden Park,) Cincinnati, O.

The school did, indeed, move to Eden Park in 1887. It stayed at this location until 2005, when it moved to a renovated facility north of the downtown area.

Circa 1907, $ 4-6

The Hebrew Union College was founded in 1875, and built on a low hill on Clifton Avenue, surrounded by beautiful grounds. It is the nation's oldest educational facility of higher learning for Jewish academic, spiritual, and professional development of Reform Judaism.

Circa 1930s, $ 4-6

The board of trustees of the college changed the name to Xavier University in 1930. Located in a suburban section of the city, Science Hall, Library Building and Hinkle Hall, shown on this postcard, were built in 1920.

Cancelled 1942, $ 3-5

This university was initially founded as the Athenaeum, a college dedicated to religion and liberal arts in 1831. In 1840, the college was renamed St. Xavier College, honoring Saint Francis Xavier who was one of the members of the Society of Jesus.

Circa 1930s, $ 3-5

Municipally owned, the fifty-acre University of Cincinnati Main Campus adjoins Burnet Woods Park. At the time of this postcard, its student body numbers were close to 12,000. Two of its buildings date back to 1819.

Circa 1930s, $ 3-5

ENGINEERING BUILDING. UNIVERSITY OF CINCINNATI, CINCINNATI, OHIO.

In 1906, the University was responsible for creating the first Cooperative Education program in the world through the College of Engineering.

Circa 1930s, $ 4-6

GENERAL VIEW OF UNIVERSITY OF CINCINNATI, CINCINNATI, OHIO.

A general view of the University of Cincinnati. The school was founded as Cincinnati College and Medical College of Ohio in 1819. It was not until 1870 that the city established the title, University of Cincinnati.

Circa 1930s, $ 4-6

UNIVERSITY OF CINCINNATI, CINCINNATI, OHIO.

In 1968, the University of Cincinnati became municipally sponsored and state-affiliated. It was noted as the second oldest and second largest university of its kind in the country.

Circa 1930s, $4-6

Hospitals

By the late 1880s, Ohio's population had grown to almost 300,000 people, and Cincinnati was noted as having the densest population of any city in the United States. At that time, there were five hospitals to accommodate that population. Pictured here in postcards are City Hospital, General Hospital, German Deaconess Hospital, Bethesda Hospital, Good Samaritan Hospital, and the Doctors Building.

Another view of City Hospital.

Cancelled 1909, $5-7

This postcard shows the Central Avenue side of City Hospital in Cincinnati.

Circa 1907, $ 5-7

An aerial view of General Hospital.

Circa 1930s, $ 4-6

General Hospital, Cincinnati, Ohio.

Another view of General Hospital.

Circa 1914, $ 4-6

German Deaconess Hospital,
Cincinnati, Ohio.

The German Deaconess Hospital.

Circa 1912, $4-6

BETHESDA HOSPITAL, CINCINNATI, OHIO

Bethesda Hospital.

Circa 1930s, $4-6

Good Samaritan Hospital.

Circa 1930s, $ 3-5

Good Samaritan Hospital, Cincinnati, Ohio

Marsh Studio

Doctors Building, 8th between Race and Vine Streets, Cincinnati, Ohio.

Doctors Building on Eighth between Race and Vine Streets.

Circa 1914, $4-6

Churches

There have always been strong religious preferences, including Catholic, Jewish, Methodist, Episcopalian, and others in the Cincinnati area. In the mid-1800s, families would often travel outside their respective neighborhoods to worship in the faith that suited them, if an appropriate venue was not close to home. Some went to local parishes, others to chapel services in Jesuit country houses or local faith-based educational institutions. But as time passed, the growing spiritual needs of communities were recognized, and churches of varied religions were established to meet the needs of the residents.

The St. Francis Church began as a small, frame church in 1819, and acted as the first organized parish to serve Irish immigrants. In 1921, it became the first cathedral in Ohio. It was decided in 1882 that the church should be moved to a new site (on Sycamore Street), but it collapsed as it progressed along the muddy streets. Though it was necessary to tear the building down, a new frame church was built – the St. Francis Xavier Church – and still stands today.

Circa 1907, $ 5-7

Francis Fortman, in 1850, donated an empty lot on the corner of Taft Road and Hackberry Street to establish a new parish dedicated to St. Francis De Sales.

Cancelled 1907, $5-7

Outgrowing the church by 1876, the parish bought land on the corner of Woodburn Avenue and Madison Road for a new parish. In 1877, the building was considered a school and the parish prepared for an even larger church.

Cancelled 1915, $ 5-7

In 1868, ground was broken to build St. Paul's Methodist Episcopal Church. Prior to the new building, from 1844-1868, the Morris Chapel stood at this location. The current structure is considered an architectural gem of the city.

Circa 1907, $ 5-7

The Calvary Church began holding Episcopal services in 1844 in a small schoolhouse in Cincinnati. Four years later, The Clifton Chapel was built on the corner of Clifton and Lafayette Avenue. Twenty years went by, and then in 1868, the present church was built on a one-acre lot that was purchased for three dollars.

Circa 1914, $ 5-7

Calvary Church, Clifton (Episcopal)—Rectory and Parish House, Cincinnati, Ohio

St. Paul Episcopal Church.

Cincinnati, O.

St. Paul Episcopal Church in Cincinnati.

Cancelled 1908, $ 5-7

No. 888. Methodist Episcopal Church, Clifton Ave., Cincinnati.

The cornerstone of the old St. Peter's Cathedral was laid in 1825.

Cancelled 1909, $3-5

ST. PETER'S CATHEDRAL, CINCINNATI, OHIO

A view of a Methodist Episcopal Church on Clifton Avenue in Cincinnati.

Circa 1930s, $ 5-7

Church of The Advent,
Kemper Lane, W. H. Cincinnati

LITERATURE HEADQUARTERS, WOMAN'S DIVISION OF CHRISTIAN SERVICE, THE METHODIST CHURCH

The Women's Division of Christian Service advocates for exploited and dispossessed individuals paying special attention to the needs of women and children. Additionally, they participate in activities that promote growth in Christianity. This postcard shows their Literature Headquarters.

Circa 1960s, $ 3-5

The 140-year-old Church of the Advent on Kemper Lane in the Walnut Hills section of Cincinnati.

Circa 1930s, $ 3-5

Hotels

The "Queen City" has been hostess to travelers from the very beginning—whether by steamer, rails, horse & buggy, or vehicle. Hotels with all the luxuries of the times are depicted in the following postcards, ranging from splendid locations for night life, entertainment, and business to lavishly decorated lobbies and indications of fire proofing for safety. It was common to see beautiful garden-scapes and dining areas fit for royalty within these grand hotels.

Both the Hotel Gibson and the Hotel Fountain Square were torn down so that the U.S. Bank Tower/Westin Hotel could be built and completed in 1981.

Circa 1914, $ 4-6

The Hotel Fountain Square in the heart of Cincinnati at Fifth and Vine Streets boasted of having 250 rooms – each having a radio. The Purple Cow Sandwich Shop was always open, offering beautiful music-box café atmosphere and delicious food.

Circa 1907, $ 4-6

Fountain Room, Hotel Gibson, Cincinnati, Ohio.

The Fountain Room at the Hotel Gibson set up for dinner guests.

Circa 1914, $ 4-6

The Grand Stairway in the Florentine Room at the Hotel Gibson.

Circa 1914, $ 4-6

GRAND STAIRWAY, FLORENTINE ROOM, HOTEL GIBSON, CINCINNATI, OHIO.

The Lee Hotel.

Circa early 1900s, $4-6

The Lee Hotel.

Dear Cousin. I am going to send you some postals now. I do not... I expect... C. S... We go every Sunday and we ... you like this card? I will ... soon. Tell Olga I will write to her soon. Edith.

Published by The Newman B...

Frederick Alms built a luxury family hotel that opened in 1891 on Victory Parkway at McMillan.

Cancelled 1948, $ 4-6

Hotel Alms   Victory Parkway at McMillan   Cincinnati, Ohio

4:-TOKYO GARDEN AND ALFRESCO DINING ROOM, ALMS HOTEL, CINCINNATI, OHIO

BROADWAY HOTEL — CINCINNATI 2, OHIO
FOURTH AND BROADWAY
ON ROUTES 25, 42, 74, 50, 27, 52, 125

SPLENDIDLY LOCATED

The lovely Tokyo Garden and Alfresco Dining Room at the Alms Hotel. The postcard notes that there are 500 rooms at the Alms and a 400-car garage. This particular scene shows the Alm's entrance to Eden Park.

Circa 1930s, $ 3-5

The Broadway Hotel provided 250 fine rooms and bachelor apartments – all with tubs and showers. The rooms were also fireproof – an important advertising fact of the day! Rates for rooms began at $3.50. The hotel also had a cocktail bar, dining room, and complete hotel services.

Circa 1930s, $ 4-6

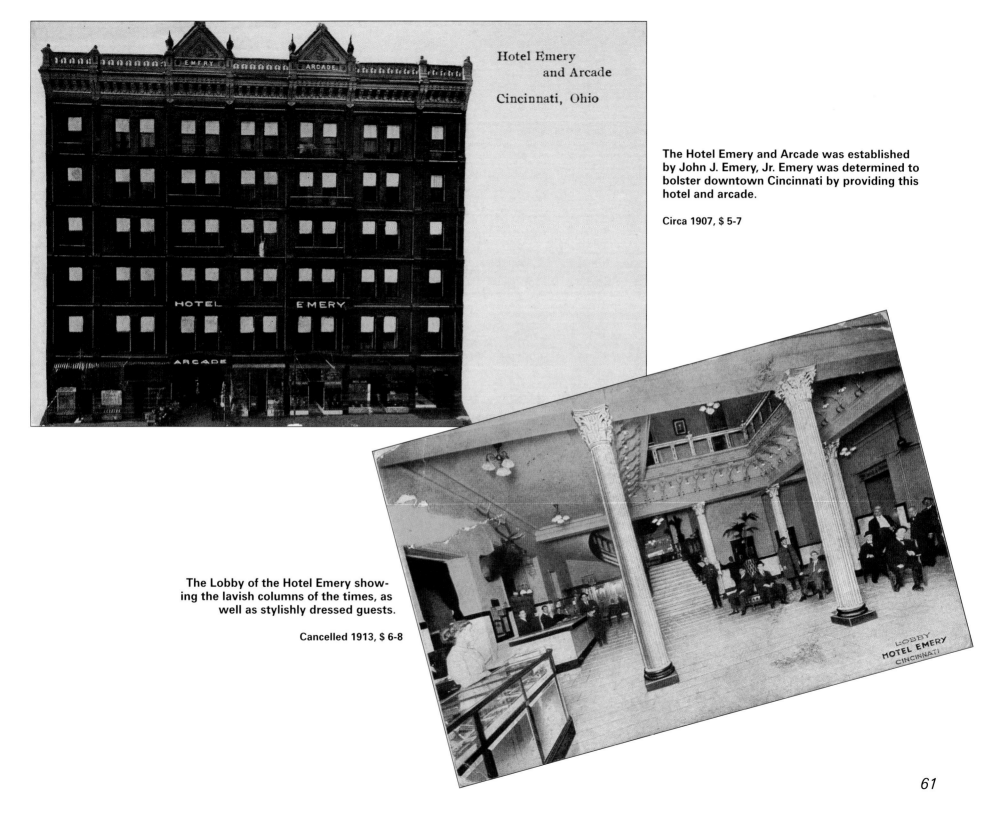

Hotel Emery
and Arcade

Cincinnati, Ohio

The Hotel Emery and Arcade was established by John J. Emery, Jr. Emery was determined to bolster downtown Cincinnati by providing this hotel and arcade.

Circa 1907, $ 5-7

The Lobby of the Hotel Emery showing the lavish columns of the times, as well as stylishly dressed guests.

Cancelled 1913, $ 6-8

1—Netherland Plaza Hotel, 5th and Race Streets, Cincinnati, Ohio

The Beautiful Hall of Mirrors, Nethe

The beautiful Hall of Mirrors inside the Netherland Plaza Hotel. Additionally, the hotel had four popular restaurants and a beautiful cocktail terrace.

Circa 1914, $ 5-7

The Netherland Plaza-Carew Tower replaced the Emery Hotel and Arcade in an effort to provide an exciting facility that offered guests, shoppers, and business people the very best services. This building and hotel is still a premier part of the Fountain Square area of Cincinnati. It was hailed as a "city within a city."

Circa 1930s, $ 5-7

Another view of the Netherland Plaza Hotel, with its 800 rooms (each supplied with a four-station radio, tub and shower, bath, and circulating ice water). Room rates began at $3.00 a day.

Cancelled 1937, $ 6-8

NETHERLAND PLAZA HOTEL, CINCINNATI

The Mariemont Inn, now run by Best Western Hotels.

Circa 1930s, $4-6

The Grand Hotel in Cincinnati.

Circa 1914, $ 5-7

86:—Grand Hotel, Cincinnati, Ohio.

The Lobby of the Grand Hotel.

Cancelled 1909, $6-8

Lobby of the Grand Hotel

78. -

The Hotel Havlin in Cincinnati. Notice the red and white striped overhangs on the upper front floors.

Cancelled 1917, $ 4-6

HOTEL HAVLIN

HOTEL HAVLIN
CINCINNATI

OXFORD HOTEL
S. E. COR. RACE AND 6TH. STS.
CINCINNATI, O.

The historic Oxford Hotel located at the southeast corner of Race and Sixth Streets in Cincinnati.

Cancelled 1917, $ 4-6

The Terrace Plaza Hotel advising the availability of 400 outside rooms, each with tub, shower, circulating ice water, and six-station radio. The entire hotel was air-conditioned and there was television available in all public rooms. Two important murals were created by Joan Miro and Saul Steinberg in 1947 for two of the four restaurants in this hotel. After the hotel was sold by builder and owner, John J. Emery, the paintings were removed. His company gave them to the Cincinnati Art Museum in 1965.

Cancelled 1954, $ 4-6

The Hotel Metropole advertising suggests, "No other hotel is better equipped to minister to the personal needs, comfort and contentment of its patrons." The staff offers modern equipment, but old-fashioned hospitality. The Metropole was the location for the Seventh World Science Fiction Convention in 1949.

Circa early 1900s, $4-6

The Hotel Sinton boasted on the front of this postcard that the hotel was fire proof and had accommodations for 1500 guests.

Circa 1914, $ 5-7

This postcard depicting the Hotel Sinton is from a "real photograph series." The hotel was torn down in 1964 so that the Provident Tower could be built.

Cancelled 1908, $ 8-10

City Streets

The city streets of Cincinnati have been bustling through the ages as people moved to and fro using varied forms of transportation. Shopping, working, entertaining, and site seeing have been important to this city and its commerce development since the 1700s. Though the streets on these cards show different times and places, the charm of Cincinnati still shines through!

For overall perspective, this postcard shows an aerial view of Cincinnati, detailing city streets, bridges, and rails.

Cancelled 1948, $ 4-6

A close-up view of the famous Fountain Square and the bronze Tyler Davidson Fountain.

Circa 1930s, $ 4-6

FOUNTAIN SQUARE BY NIGHT, CINCINNATI, OHIO.

Fountain Square by night. The Square was designated a public square in 1871.

Circa 1914, $4-6

Fourth Street looking east.

Circa early 1900s, $ 8-10

FOURTH ST. LOOKING EAST, CINCINNATI, OHIO.

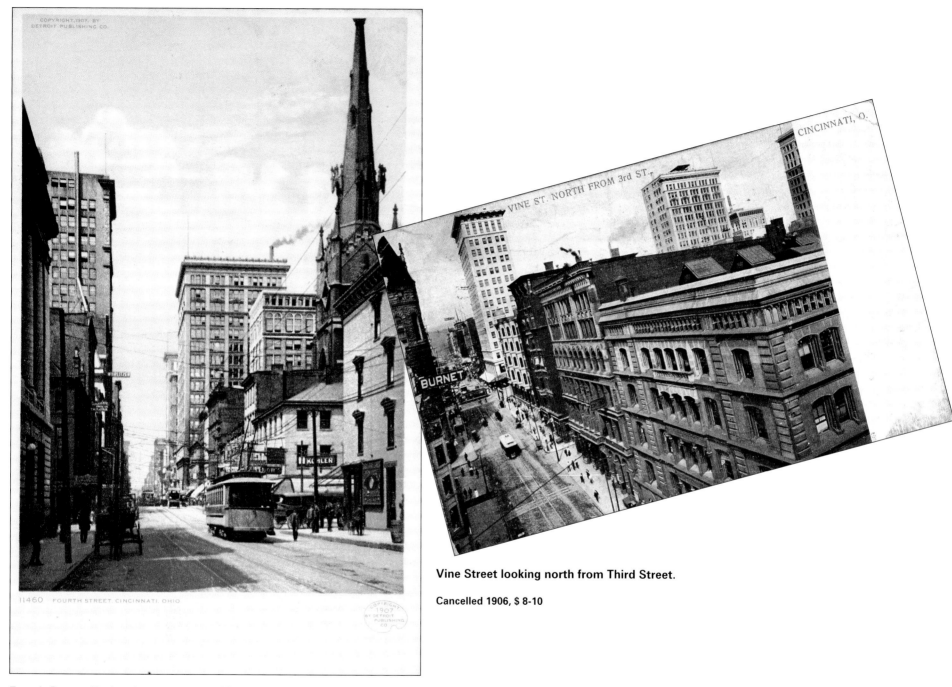

Fourth Street. Notice the streetcar and horse and buggy.

Circa 1914, $8-10

Vine Street looking north from Third Street.

Cancelled 1906, $ 8-10

Sixth Street Market House. The Sixth Street Market, built in 1895 between Plum and Western Row, was Cincinnati's largest market.

Cancelled 1900, $8-10

Sixth Street looking east from Elm Street.

Circa 1914, $8-10

A dual view: Erie Canal looking east from Plum Street, and Central Parkway Boulevard looking east from Plum Street.

Circa 1930s, $6-8

A rural road in Cincinnati near the Shelter House in Burnet Woods Park.

Cancelled 1912, $5-7

Mt. Adams Incline and Rockwood Pottery on left,
Cincinnati, Ohio

A different kind of "road." The Mt. Adams Incline is one of the several incline-
type rail services that provided transport to communities on Cincinnati hilltops.

Circa 1930s, $ 4-6

Places to Go,
Things to Do, It's Time to See!

There has been no shortage of things to do in Cincinnati throughout history! Recognizing early on that people working, living, and traveling through and around this growing town would require activities to support their busy lifestyles, Cincinnati built a thriving metropolitan capital of exciting goings-on! From history to arts and culture, and fun in the sun to relaxation in nature, this fine city has always found the best ways to live and appreciate the good life!

Fountain Square, Cincinnati, O.
Presented to the City by Henry Probasco as a Memorial to his late Brother-in-law, Mr. Tyler-Davidson.

Of course, no one visiting Cincinnati should miss viewing the Fountain Square, where the truly magnificent Tyler Davidson Fountain provides a bit of nature for a busy city.

Cancelled 1909, $ 4-6

100:-CINCINNATI ART MUSEUM: EDEN PARK: CINCINNATI, OHIO.

The Cincinnati Art Museum was founded in 1881, and opened its doors in 1886. It was called by many, "The Art Palace of the West."

Cancelled 1955, $4-6

The museum's foyer art. In 1993, the foyer – called the Great Hall – was restored. The original 1886 columns and stone arch were uncovered after more than forty years.

Cancelled 1910, $ 4-6

FOYER, ART MUSEUM, CINCINNATI, O.

Music Hall,
Cincinnati, Ohio.

Soldiers kept here, turned into Hospital

The Cincinnati Music Hall was built in 1878 with money raised from what is
believed to be the nation's first matching grant funding initiative.

Cancelled 1918, $ 5-7

6631 MUSIC HALL FROM WASHINGTON PARK, CINCINNATI, OHIO.

Beautifully landscaped, the Music Hall has been updated and renovated over the years to be one of the most beautiful halls in the nation.

Circa early 1900s, $ 5-7

3—Ault Park, Shelter House, Cincinnati, Ohio

3A-H289

The Shelter House at Ault Park. Today, the Cincinnati Horticulture Society holds a spectacular flower show in the park.

Circa 1930s, $ 4-6

and Music Hall, Cincinnati, O.

Washington Park is located at Elm, Race, and Twelfth Streets and can be seen from the Music Hall.

Cancelled 1909, $ 5-7

An aerial view of Ault Park, named after Ida May Ault and Levi Addison Ault who were active in Cincinnati park development. The first tract of land, consisting of 142 acres (as well as other tracts later), was a gift to the city of Cincinnati from the Ault family.

Circa 1930s, $ 3-5

Glimpse of Eden Park, Cincinnati, Ohio.

Elsinore Tower, Eden Park, Cincinnati, O.

Eden Park's Elsinore Tower was built in 1883 to memorialize a Shakespeare Festival that was being held in the city.

Cancelled 1908, $ 3-5

Eden Park is a prominent part of Cincinnati's love for nature. There are over 186 acres of parkland, brought together through a chain of purchases beginning in 1859. The name heralds from the Garden of Eden. The Cincinnati Art Museum, Cincinnati Art Academy, the Irwin M. Krohn Conservatory, Playhouse in the Park, and the Murray Seasongood Pavilion can all be found in Eden Park.

Circa 1914, $ 3-5

Another view of the Elsinore Tower at the Eden Park Entrance located at Gilbert Avenue and Elsinore Place.

Circa 1914, $ 3-5

ELSINORE ENTRANCE, EDEN PARK, CINCINNATI, OHIO.

EDEN PARK ENTRANCE BRIDGE, CINCINNATI, OHIO.

The Eden Park Entrance Bridge.

Circa 1930s, $3-5

The main entrance to Eden Park.

Circa 1930s, $ 3-5

10335. MAIN ENTRANCE, EDEN PARK, CINCINNATI, O.

Lakes of East Eden Park.

Cancelled 1938, $ 2-4

LAKES OF EAST EDEN PARK, CINCINNAT...

E-453

The Eden Park Conservatory contains a fern house, a display house where specimen-blooming plants are exhibited, and a palm house with cascades and streams of flowing water.

Circa 1930s, $ 3-5

View of Eden Park Conservatory, Cincinnati, Ohio — D-7

81

The Cactus House in the Irwin M. Krohn Conservatory. The Krohn Conservatory is the third greenhouse in Eden Park, opened to the public in 1933.

Circa early 1900s, $ 3-5

WATER TOWER, EDEN PARK, CINCINNATI, OHIO

1236

The Eden Park Water Tower was completed in 1894 and is 172 feet high. The City now uses the tower as a communications facility.

Cancelled 1938, $ 3-5

Eden Park Reservoir, (Baker's Pass,) Cincinnati, O.

The old reservoir in Eden Park dates back to 1866.

Circa early 1900s, $3-5

Another view of the Eden Park Waterworks.

Cancelled 1909, $3-5

A view of the Ohio River from Eden Park's horticultural buildings.

Circa 1907, $3-5

Coney Island in Cincinnati was a famed amusement park regarded as one of the top in the nation. In 1870, James Parker (an apple farmer) was approached by a group who wanted to use his 400-tree, 20-acre orchard for a private picnic. The idea for an amusement park was born! Parker added a mule-powered merry-go-round, a dance hall, and a dining hall. As his apple trees died, he replaced them with shade trees that guests would appreciate.

Circa 1940s, $15-17

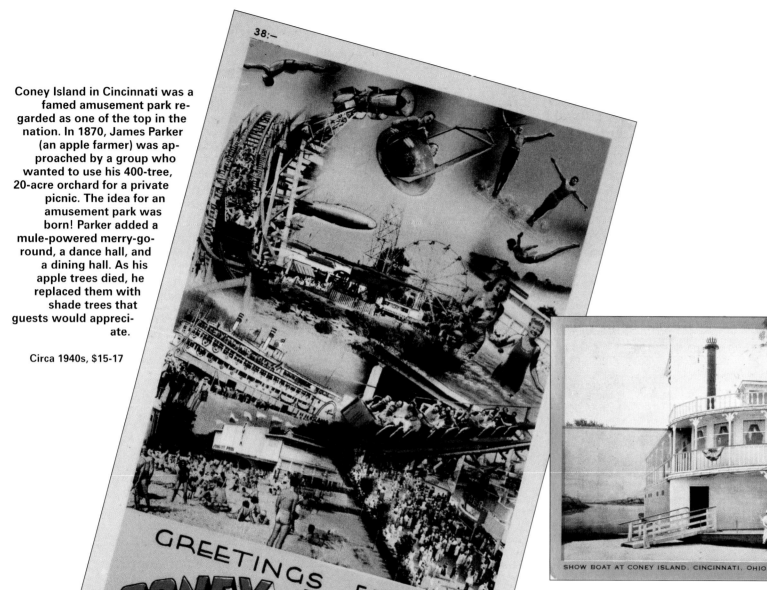

SHOW BOAT AT CONEY ISLAND, CINCINNATI, OHIO   E-863

The first group wanting to rent Parker's land had intended to hire a riverboat to bring their party to the picnic spot. Because of this, Parker saw the value in becoming involved with steamers for entertainment rather than merely transportation for commerce. So, in 1886, Parker made the decision to sell his land to a group headed by two steamboat captains who wanted to encourage steamer travel. The park was renamed "Ohio Grove, The Coney Island of the West," as a hopeful link to the famed New York park.

Cancelled 1938, $13-15

Island Queen Landing at Coney Island, Cincinnati, Ohio

Though the first steamer to carry passengers was named, *The Guiding Star*, in 1886, the famous *Island Queen* began service in 1896 in this increasingly popular park.

Circa 1914, $13-15

12—Coney Island Steamer "Island Queen", Cincinnati, Ohio

The *Island Queen* was one of the largest river excursion steamers in the world. It was made of all steel, was glass-enclosed, and smokeless. It's ballroom deck approximated 20,000 square feet of hardwood floor, cushioned on a specially designed air chamber.

Circa 1930s, $10-12

11—Sunlite Pool, Coney Island, Cincinnati, Ohio

Coney Island

This postcard of the Sunlite Pool at Coney Island lets readers know that the park had the largest re-circulating water pool in America. The pool is 200 x 401 feet in dimension, and the water depth ranges from six inches to ten and one half feet. There is a 3,500,000 water gallon capacity, which is cooled to a refreshing temperature in hot weather. Its filtration plant is adequate to meet the requirements of a city with a population of 200,000.

Circa 1930s, $12-14

A night scene of the swimming pool at Coney Island.

Cancelled 1938, $12-14

NIGHT SCENE OF SWIMMING POOL AT CONEY ISLAND, CINCINNATI, OHIO

1195

Ohio River Regatta, Cincinnati, O.

An exciting Ohio River Regatta!

Cancelled 1911, $6-8

ENTRANCE TO ZOOLOGICAL GARDENS, CINCINNATI, OHIO

In 1875, the Zoological Garden opened its doors to the public with a small number of exhibited animals. There were great financial difficulties over the years and, though they were able to resist bankruptcy in 1898, still had to create ideas that would allow the zoo to stay open. At one point, one hundred Sioux Native Americans were invited to create and live in a village on the zoo property in hopes that this would increase visitors wanting to understand Indian life. After three months, this plan failed. The city bought the zoo in 1932.

Circa 1930s, $ 7-9

A Main Walk in the Zoo Park. Now renamed the Cincinnati Zoo and Botanical Garden, it ranks among the top five zoos in the United States.

Circa early 1900s, $5-7

A Main Walk in the Zoo Park, Cincinnati, O.

The birdcages at the Zoo.

Cancelled 1910, $6-8

The Reptile House.

Circa 1914, $ 5-7

REPTILE HOUSE, ZOOLOGICAL GARDENS, CINCINNATI, OHIO

F-158

Herbivora Building, Zoo Garden, Cincinnati O.

The Herbivora Building.

Cancelled 1910, $ 6-8

The Monkey House.

Cancelled 1910, $6-8

MONKEY HOUSE, ZOOLOGICAL GARDEN, CINCINNATI, O.

THE KEMPER LOG CABIN – CIN'TI, ZOO.

The Kemper Log Cabin was built in 1804 by Reverend James Kemper. The cabin was moved from Kemper Lane in Walnut Hills to the Zoological Garden in 1913 by the Patriotic Society of Cincinnati.

Circa 1907, $ 6-8

PARLOR BED

This is the Parlor Bedroom style of 1804 seen inside the Kemper Log Cabin. When the cabin was moved to the Zoological Garden, it was taken apart log by log and reassembled at the new site.

Circa 1914, $ 5-7

This is the four-poster and trundle bed with log cabin quilts of that period. The Kemper Log Cabin was noted as the oldest house standing within the Miami Purchase.

Circa 1914, $5-7

FOUR POSTER AND TRUNDLE BEDS WITH LOG CABIN QUILTS OF THAT PERIOD   2B218

"IN THE STRETCH," LATONIA RACE TRACK, CINCINNATI, OHIO, No. 62.

Though there was much controversy regarding the completion times for the Latonia Race Track, the first horse meets ran in June of 1883. The new track was deemed a great success.

Cancelled 1911, $ 8-10

VIEW FROM MT. ADAMS, CAREW TOWER AND UNION CENTRAL LIFE BUILDING IN DISTANCE.

View of the city's high-rise towers from Mt. Adams. Mt. Adams is a historic community named after President John Quincy Adams. Community living in Cincinnati has always given residents a bit of "the best from both worlds" – the relaxed community setting with great neighborhoods and friendly small-town encounters and the convenience of big city life and commerce filled with the significant cultural perks of downtown life.

Circa 1930s, $ 3-5

Fort Thomas Drill Grounds in Cincinnati. In 1877, Fort Thomas was chosen by the United States Army as a military post. Its beautiful landscaping and lovely highlands overlooking the Ohio River was part of the reasoning for the choice.

Cancelled 1907, $ 4-6

In Piatt Park, at Garfield Place and Vine Street, stands the James A. Garfield Monument honoring the twentieth U.S. President, who was sworn into office in 1881. Garfield was shot in July of the same year by an assassin and died in September of that year. The statue was originally placed in the middle of Vine Street, but was moved to Piatt Park when it caused traffic issues in the 1900s.

Cancelled 1906, $4-6

The Taft Museum, one of the finest small art museums in the United States, is a National Historic Landmark in Cincinnati. Built in 1820, it includes almost 700 works of art.

Circa early 1900s, $ 4-6

Taft Residence, 4th and Pike Sts., Cincinnati, O.

Formerly the residence of Mr. and Mrs. Charles P. Taft, the building was restored as closely as possible to its original form. The family donated the fine art, and the residence, to the Cincinnati Institute of Fine Arts.

Cancelled 1910, $ 4-6

The Yellow Room in the Taft Museum. The artwork in the museum ranges from European and American master paintings to Chinese porcelains and European decorative arts.

Circa 1914, $ 3-5

Mecklenburg's Garden was established in 1865. The garden held ritual celebrations up until World War II to choose the "Mayor of Kloppenburg." This surname, *Kloppenburg,* was selected because of the sound made as an empty stein banged onto the table – signaling refills. One of the ritual's more serious functions was to introduce German immigrants to American politics.

Circa early 1900s, $ 4-6

MECKLENBURG'S GARDEN, Cincinnati, Ohio   *Established* 1865

1679   Rookwood Pottery, Cincinnati, O.   James K. Stewart, Pub.

Rockwood Pottery was established in 1880 when Maria Longworth formed the business after being snubbed by female members of another pottery club. Her father purchased an old schoolhouse for her to build a thriving pottery business. In 1892, the pottery business was moved to Mt. Adams, which is atop a large hill.

Circa early 1900s, $5-7

The Mt. Adams Incline. In 1880, the incline was adapted to move streetcars. The famous Rookwood Pottery, though not visible, would be situated just to the left of the incline on this postcard.

Circa 1907, $ 5-7

Rookwood Pottery, Cincinnati, Ohio.

MT. ADAMS INCLINE, CINCINNATI, O.

67002

The Rookwood Pottery won awards in very prestigious international competitions while most artists in Cincinnati were still in their formative years. Maria Longworth worked hard, taking pottery from a hobby to a business. She was successful in making Rookwood Pottery one of the nation's first major industries to be owned and operated by a woman.

Cancelled 1912, $ 4-6

There were five incline railways (also called funicular railways) that served the surrounding hilltop communities of Cincinnati. Mt. Adams Incline was opened in 1875. This was the last incline to remain in service, closing in 1948.

Cancelled 1909, $4-6

To assist travelers, the Mt. Adams & Eden Park Inclined Railway Company opened a connecting horse and carriage line from downtown Cincinnati to the bottom of the incline in 1877.

Circa 1914, $ 5-7

Another view of the Price Hill Incline, which was noted as the steepest grade for an incline at 44.6 degrees.

Cancelled 1911, $ 4-6

The Price Hill Incline, opened in 1875, was located on Eighth Street.

Circa 1914, $ 4-6

Bellevue Incline, Cincinnati, O.

In 1876, the Bellevue Incline was built because the Cincinnati communities of Clifton Heights, University Heights, and Fairview were in need of transportation via an incline railway.

Cancelled 1909, $4-6

More Faces of Cincinnati

Take a look at some of the random faces of Cincinnati—a little more of everything! Inclines to arcades; buildings to landscapes; steamers to churches!

The west end of Cincinnati from Price Hill.

Cancelled 1911, $ 4-6

WEST END FROM PRICE HILL CINCINNATI, O.

PHOTO BY LA

SKYLINE AND OHIO RIVER, CINCINNATI, OHIO

3A-H284

The skyline of Cincinnati from the Ohio River.

Cancelled 1941, $ 3-5

Vine Street, looking south from Sixth Street.

Cancelled 1928, $ 5-7

Downtown Cincinnati, East Fifth Street – note the United States Post Office on the left.

Cancelled 1952, $ 4-6

East Walnut Hills — a suburb of Cincinnati. Residents across Cincinnati often described the varied small towns and communities of the city as a way to have a "big city with a small-town feel." With many of the residential neighborhoods springing up from the early nineteenth century, it's easy to see why the city retains its charm, even to this day.

Circa early 1900s, $ 4-6

The Suspension Bridge.

Cancelled 1939, $ 3-5

SUSPENSION BRIDGE ACROSS THE OHIO RIVER, CINCINNATI, OHIO.

A view of The Suspension Bridge across the Ohio River.

Circa early 1900s, $3-5

Skyline of Cincinnati, Ohio

Skyline of Cincinnati.

Circa 1930s, $3-5

Arcade. Cincinnati, O.

The Arcade in Cincinnati.

Circa early 1900, $ 5-7

The Ohio River from Eden Park.

Circa 1914, $ 3-5

OHIO RIVER FROM EDEN PARK, CINCINNATI, OHIO.

Herbivora Building at the Zoo, Cincinnati, Ohio.

The Herbivora Building at the Zoo.

Circa early 1900s, $4-6

In Cincinnati's history, nature was not always a kind mother. Great devastation — city and lives — took place as is depicted by this postcard showing floodwaters at Eighth and McClean Ave

Circa 1913, $12-14

Q. & C. Terminal 8th. and McClean Ave. during Great Flood 1913 Cincinnati, Ohio.

Ohio River Flood, January, 1937
6. Suspension Bridge, Cincinnati, Ohio

In the Ohio River Flood of 1937, flood levels reached almost eighty feet.

Circa early 1900s, $7-9

Though the postcard advises that a tornado struck on July 7th, 1915, some historical accounts speak of a vicious wind and rainstorm. It was considered, since there were no reports of tornadoes and the damage was all moving in one direction, that the high wind was the result of thunderstorm microbursts and not by tornado. Regardless, destruction was massive.

Circa 1915, $12-14

TORNADO JULY 7TH 1915. CINCINNATI, O. 6TH & MOUND STS.

Another photo postcard of the devastation from the July 7th, 1915, storm incident at Sixth and Mound Streets.

Circa 1915, $14-16

Though from the postcard it is unclear about exactly what type of devastation has made it's way to *Charles Street looking north*, the message on the card suggests that a fire struck sometime in early 1904.

Circa early 1900s, $9-11

16—U. S. Post Office, Cincinnati, Ohio

The United States Post Office.

Circa 1930s, $4-6

The General Hospital, completed in 1911 and noted as having a capacity for 925 patients.

Cancelled 1939, $4-6

SPITAL, CINCINNATI, OHIO

IB-H1709

Another view of the Taft Museum with hours and rates.

Cancelled 1939, $ 4-6

THE TAFT MUSEUM, CINCINNATI, OHIO.   OPEN FREE: WEEK-DAYS 10 TO 5, SUNDAYS 2 TO 6

The First National Bank building located at Fourth and Walnut.

Circa 1910, $5-7

FIRST NATIONAL BANK
4TH & WALNUT CINCINNATI, O.

The Traction Building at Fifth and Walnut Streets.

Cancelled 1911, $ 5-7

The Union Trust Building.

Circa 1914, $4-6

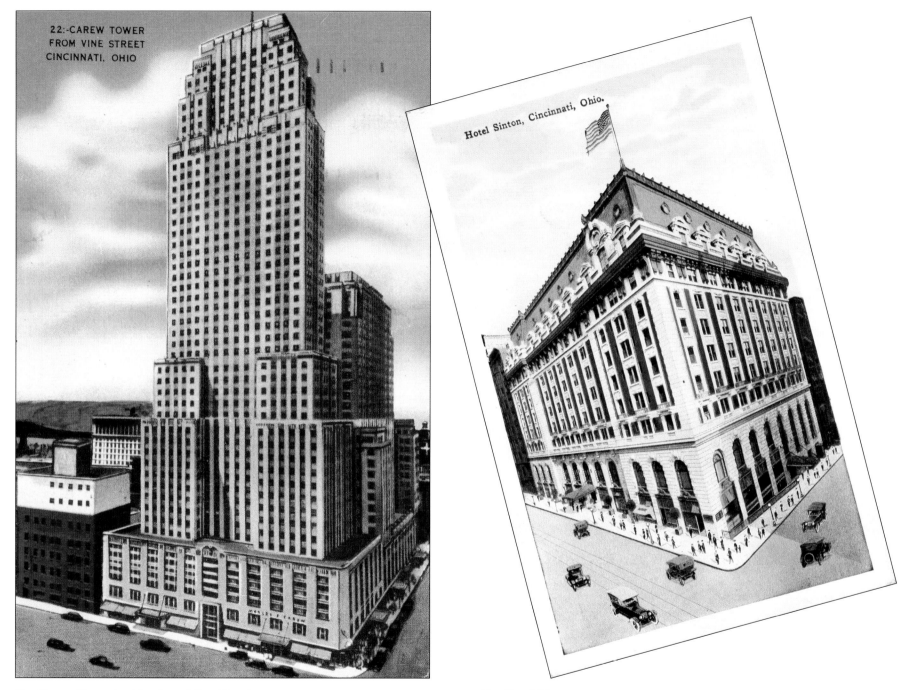

22:-CAREW TOWER
FROM VINE STREET
CINCINNATI, OHIO

Hotel Sinton, Cincinnati, Ohio.

The Carew Tower looking from Vine Street.

Cancelled 1958, $4-6

The Hotel Sinton.

Circa 1914, $4-6

The Netherland Plaza and Terrace Plaza Hotels.

Circa 1914, $4-6

Another view of the Netherland Hilton. This card advises that there is teletype capability at the hotel.

Cancelled 1959, $4-6

HOTEL ALMS

WALNUT HILLS,   CINCINNATI, OHIO

The Hotel Alms in Walnut Hills.

Circa 1907, $4-6

Hotel Gibson and Fountain Square, Cincinnati, Ohio

The Hotel Gibson and Fountain Square.

Circa 1914, $ 4-6

Sheraton-Gibson Hotel, Cincinnati, Ohio
ON HISTORIC FOUNTAIN SQUARE

The Gibson Hotel, on this card, labeled as the Sheraton-Gibson on historic Fountain Square.

Circa 1930s, $4-6

Sheraton-Gibson Hotel, Cincinnati, Ohio ON HISTORIC FOUNTAIN SQUARE

Another view of the Sheraton-Gibson Hotel with a clear view of the fountain at Fountain Square.

Cancelled 1955, $4-6

NEW UNION CENTRAL LIFE
INSURANCE CO. BLDG.
CINCINNATI, OHIO.

A. O. KRAEMER, Pub., Cin'ti, O.

View No. 196 — Music Hall — Cincinnati, O.

The Music Hall.

Circa early 1900s, $5-7

A night scene of the New Union Central Life Insurance Company
building.

Cancelled 1917, $ 5-7

118

WITHROW HIGH SCHOOL, CINCINNATI, OHIO.

Withrow High School.

Circa 1930s, $ 4-6

Art Museum and Academy, Cincinnati, O., under the management of Cincinnati Art Museum Association

The Art Museum and Academy under the management of the Cincinnati Art Museum Association.

Cancelled 1908, $4-6

120

Hughes High School.

Cancelled 1928, $4-6

Lane Seminary in Walnut Hills held debates about slavery in 1834 for eighteen consecutive nights. Because of the way this affected the nation's thinking about slavery, the results of these discussions brought forth an immediate call for abolition.

Cancelled 1912, $5-7

No. 550. Lane Seminary, Walnut Hills, Cincinnati.

OHIO MECHANICS' INSTITUTE, CINCINNATI, OHIO.

The Ohio Mechanics' Institute.

Circa early 1900s, $4-6

Fern Bank Dam and Locks, Ohio River, Cincinnati, Ohio.

66879

Fern Bank Dam and Locks, Ohio River, in Cincinnati.

Cancelled 1916, $3-5

Fernbank Dam, near Cincinnati, O.
Showing Locks (on left) with Upper Gate Closed and Water Passing over Wickets.

Fernbank Dam, showing the locks with the upper gate closed and water passing over wickets.

Circa early 1900s, $ 3-5

A newer riverboat view.

Circa 1960s, $ 5-7

A newer Cincinnati.

Circa 1960s, $4-6

Bibliography

Cincinnati Art Museum. "History of the Museum."
http://www.cincinnatiartmuseum.org. 04/13/06.
Cincinnati, Ohio Government. "City of Cincinnati."
http://www.cincinnati-oh.gov. 04/13/06.
Cincinnati Regional Chamber of Commerce. " Cincinnati USA Regional Chamber
    History." http://www.gccc.com. 04/13/06.
Coney Island Park. "Plan a Visit—History."
http://www.coneyislandpark.com. 04/13/06
Hamilton County Sheriff's Office. "The Cincinnati Workhouse."
http://www.hcso.org. 04/13/06.
Mount Adams Today. "Mt. Adams History."
http://www.mtadamstoday.com/. 03/28/06.
Ohio Historical Society. "Cincinnati."
http://www.ohiohistorycentral.org. 03/28/06.
Ohio Historical Society. "Ohio History."
http://www.ohiohistory.org. 04/13/06.
Reed, Robert. *Greetings From Ohio: Vintage Postcards*. Pennsylvania: Schiffer
Publishing, Ltd., 2003.
Wikipedia, the Free Encyclopedia. "Cincinnati, Ohio."
http://en.wikipedia.org. 03/28/06.
Wikitravel. "Cincinnati." http://wikitravel.org. 03/28/06.
Winckler, Suzanne. *The Smithsonian Guide to Historic America—The Great Lakes
States.* New York: Stewart, Tabori & Chang, 1989.
YMCA. "150 Years in YMCA History 1851-2001."
http://www.ecymca.org. 04/13/06.

PUBLIC LIBRARY, CINCINNATI, OHIO.

Index